Journey to Soul

LESSONS TO HELP YOU ESTABLISH A SPIRITUAL PRACTICE, RECONNECT WITH YOUR INTUITION, AND OPEN UP TO THE DIVINE FEMININE.

COURTNEY TIFFANY

First paperback edition June 2020

Book cover design by Mandi Lynn
Book interior design by Ines Monnet/Ines | Book Formatter

Paperback ISBN: 978-1-7349209-1-8
Ebook ISBN: 978-1-7349209-0-1

www.courtneytiffany.com

To those forging their own path

Contents

Introduction

*J*ourney to Soul first came about as a way for me to organize all I had learned during my spiritual awakening. It was an accumulation of everything I had learned during the two years of my journey toward self-discovery that I could turn into something beneficial for others.

I first created a self-paced online course titled "Journey to Soul" back in the spring of 2019. I wanted to create something women could do on their own, when it best suited them, so they could understand themselves better. I, myself, had a spiritual awakening after my second child was born just thirteen short months after my first.

I was at a point in my life where all I was doing was feeding babies, changing diapers, and waking up every two hours to rock someone back to sleep—or at least that's what it felt like at the time. It was 2016, and I was consumed by motherhood, eventually getting to a point where I didn't know who I was as an individual anymore. All I knew was this new role I had taken on as a mother. I had gone from working full time to being a full-time, stay-at-home mom. I was not only having trouble adjusting to my new schedule but adjusting to my new identity.

I had left the best job I ever had to stay home with my two young children, spending most of my time indoors because carting two young children around town by myself was very overwhelming.

I love being a mother and I adore my children, but I felt like something was missing from my life. I didn't want my entire life to revolve around my children. I know many women who would be satisfied with that life and might judge me for saying this, but I wanted my life to be so much more than just being a mom. I was still an individual and had hopes and dreams for my future.

I remember the day I hit rock bottom in August 2017. My husband came home from work and found me curled up, bawling my eyes out on our bedroom floor. I felt like I couldn't go on. I was in the darkest of places and couldn't see any light at the end of the tunnel. I felt trapped, and I knew if I didn't get help for my postpartum depression, things would only continue to get worse. I told him what I had been going through and that I needed help.

The next day, I called a therapist who specialized in postpartum depression and booked an appointment. During my sessions, she helped me realize I was giving all of my time and energy to those in my family who needed me, my husband included, and that left me with nothing to give to myself. I had to learn to fill my cup first so I could eventually give myself to others. That meant finding a babysitter, asking for help, and stepping away every now and then to be alone. And with some adjustments, I did just that.

Around the same time as my breakdown, I started listening to a podcast by Sabrina Domenosky called *Rewilding for Women*. She talked about wild women, the divine feminine, and sisterhood, and it was exactly the medicine I needed. She just so happened to be hosting a live event in Sedona a couple months later, so I quickly signed myself up. That weekend was my first weekend away since my children were born!

Surrounded by fifty other women, I dove deep into the many facets of femininity. That retreat lit my soul on fire. I knew things were starting to change in my life, and my old way of doing things was no longer going to work. I spent a lot of time that year journaling, meditating, learning astrology and tarot, and working on my own healing journey. I healed a lot of ancestral and karmic wounds I had been holding on to, and I released the negativity and anger I had been building up.

After the retreat, I made a commitment to start taking care of myself and my needs. I started to live my life more authentically and more in tune with who I wanted to be as a person and what I felt was right. I started using my voice and working on clearing my throat chakra so I could speak my truth. I learned to open my heart, fill my cup, and then let it spill over and spread love to others. I focused on building a community of sisterhood and surrounding myself with amazing women I could lean on in times of need and who respected and supported me no matter what.

In the last four years, my life has drastically changed for the better, which is what prompted me to create "Journey to Soul." And now, I want to share it with you in this easy-to-digest format.

Inside this book, you'll find twenty-one different lessons to read, preferably over the next twenty-one days. I want you to allow the messages of each lesson to soak in and marinate. You might need time to reflect upon something you've read so it can really resonate with you and be applied to your own life. Besides, experts say it takes at least twenty-one days to build a new habit, and that's what we are doing here. We are creating new daily habits that will help you get in touch with your soul, increase your intuition, and reestablish your spiritual self.

The modern world we live in is crazy hectic. There are constantly screens in our faces, noises in our ears, smells of pollution, and long lists of things to do. It's no wonder we have the highest levels of anxiety and depression ever recorded. While our technology has created some amazing advancements and made our lives a lot easier, it has also harmed us just the same.

We need to learn how to deal with the things that are constantly coming at us, and we need to learn how to cope with the pressures of daily life in a healthy way that works best for us. We need to get back in touch with our souls and do what feels right without being swayed by current societal norms.

I encourage you to grab a notebook as you read a chapter each day and write down your answers to the reflection questions. Take the time to get to know yourself again. Learn what makes your inner flame spark, release the old habits and patterns that no longer serve you, and grow as an individual so you can be the person you really are or who you want to become. Face your shadows, allow yourself to feel your emotions, and heal. I believe we can heal and grow through self-discovery.

It's important to note here that you are only going to get out of this journey what you put into it. If you want to skim the book and pick up pieces here and there, that's fine. But if you really want to go on a transformational journey of self-discovery, I suggest you find the time each day to do the work. We have to hold ourselves accountable if we want to change how we live our lives. Repeat the affirmations, reflect, and answer the questions, and really take everything you are reading to your own inner flame. Recognize your strengths and weaknesses, understand where you need to grow, let go of what is hindering you from that growth, and become the best version of yourself.

Within each chapter, you will see a daily affirmation. I encourage you to write these down somewhere you will see them throughout the day. Repeat them out loud (yes, out loud) to yourself in the mirror, in the car, or in the drive-thru line. When we start speaking affirmations, it helps us rewire our brain. We start to believe the things we are saying and incorporate more confidence and positivity into our day. You can even change your phone's background to your affirmation, grab a dry erase marker and write it on your bathroom mirror, or write it on a slip of paper and carry it with you in your pocket or purse.

This is your time to take a journey back to your soul. Find your authentic voice and start living your truth.

Lesson 1

Creating a Daily Practice

Today's Affirmation:

I have the freedom and power
to create the life I love.

Today, we are starting things off easy. This is all about carving out the time each day to complete these lessons. Take a look at your schedule and see what time of day would work best for you to commit to reading and answering the reflection questions. Perhaps waking up thirty minutes early to get in that quiet time before the rest of your household wakes up is best. Or maybe you are a night owl and would like to read before bed. If that's the case, read Lesson 1 at night and implement it the next day. It doesn't really matter how or when you do this; all that matters is that you make the time because, really, you are making time for yourself. You are making time to reflect, turn inward, and find peace, clarity, and insight. The only way to make changes is by doing different things. We will never progress forward if we keep doing the same things we've always done.

Remember, we are only making a commitment for twenty-one days. That's not even an entire month, although, ideally, you'll find some helpful things in this book and will adapt them into your daily living, even after you've finished reading.

After all, that's what we want. We want to build new habits. We want to challenge our way of thinking and become better people. Everyone on this planet wants more or better for themselves; they want to be the best they can be. That is human nature. But we tend to make excuses for ourselves and give up before we really even get started. Even if you start with just fifteen minutes of quiet time each day, that's better than nothing.

These next few weeks are all about self-love and self-discovery, uncovering our truths. We are striving to live a more authentic life, meaning we don't wear masks and we don't run and hide from our thoughts and feelings. Today, we are simply getting to know what makes us feel good, what lights us up, and what we're passionate about. When we take the time to do the things we love—whether that's painting, writing, or starting a business— we tend to be happier. Think about the topics you could go on and on talking about. What do you find yourself researching when you have downtime? Those are the hobbies or activities you should invest more of your time into.

I encourage anyone who finds themselves constantly complaining or having negative thoughts about themselves, their situation, or others to start a gratitude journal. Is your money tight? Are you constantly stressed out? Do your coworkers suck? I've been there. I encourage you to write down three things you are grateful for every day. It could be as simple as food in your belly or as specific as a beautiful moment you shared with a loved one. It doesn't matter. When we start writing down our lists of gratitude, it reminds us to be grateful for what we already have. This, in return, allows us to open ourselves up to receive more— more abundance, more love, and more prosperity. When you are appreciative of the people and things in your life, the universe tends to send more good things your way. It's based on the frequency you are emitting.

On top of gratitude lists, the biggest and most transformative thing I've done in my life is develop a daily spiritual practice. I've even started sharing those intimate moments on my Instagram stories in hopes of inspiring others to do the same. Taking anywhere from five to fifteen minutes out of my day to check in with myself, ask for guidance, journal, or pull an oracle card or two has made all the difference for me. It's during this time that I fill my cup. I can clear away any emotions that arise during my day. I am able to re-center. I'm able to find clarity or solace when I'm in a confusing time in my life.

When I bring up my spiritual practice, people immediately think I'm meditating all the time, and while sometimes I am, that's not always the case. It depends on what I need in that moment. My spiritual practice changes daily because my needs are different every day.

Some days, I'm so in my head, overanalyzing everything, that I make it a point to focus on grounding myself during my daily practice. Simply sitting on the ground and tapping into the earth beneath me provides enough relief. Or I'll try some embodiment work, where I literally get out of my head and just move my body.

Meditation doesn't always have to be about clearing your mind. I like to see where the energy takes me. I might meditate and ask questions to my spirit guides to see if I get an immediate response. Sometimes they aren't always forthcoming, so I'll ask them to send me a sign during the day.

I've meditated on ascending deep into outer space, I've drawn energy from the earth's core, and I've even pictured myself scaling a volcano with Pele, the great Hawaiian goddess of fire.

Meditation isn't always about emptying your mind, unless you want that sort of thing. For me, it's about going deeper, exploring the mysteries within my mind and the cosmos.

If you have never tried meditation, do a simple YouTube search and find a guided meditation or go to www.lifein-alignment.com and download one for free.

When you are being guided by a meditation, a few minutes can pass by so quickly, and you'll usually feel lighter and less stressed afterward. There are guided meditations for all sorts of things: to reduce stress, to connect with your higher self, to connect with a specific god/goddess, to balance your chakras, the list goes on. Find one that calls to you in the moment, whatever sparks your interest. You never have to try something new on your own. We hardly ever succeed that way.

Find an app or a person to help you. Find an accountability partner if you need one. But just start checking in with yourself today and figuring out what you need in this very moment in time.

Reflection Questions:

◊ List three things you are grateful for in this moment.

◊ What is it you love to do?

◊ What brings you joy?

◊ What do you wish you could spend more time doing?

◊ What is something you've always wanted to try?

◊ Now that you've identified those things, how can you fit that into your schedule over the next couple of weeks?

Lesson 2

Manifesting Who You Want to Be

Today's Affirmation:

My thoughts become my reality.

Manifesting in the simplest of terms is writing down and visualizing your goals. It's about turning your thoughts and dreams into reality. The best time to do this is during the new moon. The new moon is the beginning of the next lunar cycle, indicating a fresh start.

We can manifest or set new intentions during this time to give ourselves something to focus on. It's something to strive for, for we all want to be the best versions of ourselves we can be. We all like to make New Year's resolutions but tend to forget about them by February. I've always liked the idea of focusing on one thing at a time. So, what if we made a new resolution every twenty-eight days? This could help us break things down into smaller, more achievable goals. Of course, not every goal will be achieved in one month, but you can start laying the groundwork right away to make it happen. By taking small, achievable steps, we can bring ourselves that much closer to our goals.

Picture yourself successful, enjoying life, and being the best version of you. What does that look like? How does it make you feel? What sort of things would you be enjoying?

When we visualize ourselves achieving our goals, it's the same as actually doing them; our brains don't know the difference. Allow yourself to really soak up the moment. When you visualize, allow your emotions to swell up so you can actually experience those feelings of accomplishment and satisfaction. See yourself standing on stage in front of a crowd. Picture yourself crossing the finish line. Imagine how it would feel accomplishing that one thing you've always dreamed of.

Think about this for a moment: Our present-day circumstances are an accumulation of our past thoughts and actions. If you want a different future, you have to start making changes today. How does the best version of yourself behave? What habits can you develop that will help you be successful?

I had a coach mention to me once that she would write down all her goals for the year and put them in a jar at her desk. Every day, she would pull one slip of paper and visualize herself accomplishing that goal, and by the end of the year, she had accomplished nine out of the twelve goals she had written down, with the others in the works as well!

It's important we get super clear on who we want to be and what we want to do. If you see yourself in a different career or living abroad, what small steps can you take to make that possible? I'm not talking about creating a vision board and letting it gather dust in the corner. I'm talking about writing down your goals, constantly reminding yourself of them, feeling into them, visualizing yourself achieving them, and turning them into your reality.

You must understand that everything is energy. Everything in nature, including us, is made up of energetic currents, and in any given moment, we all put out and receive energetic vibrations. This is why you may feel upbeat and happy after hanging around a cheerful person. And vice versa, you might avoid hanging with friends who like to complain and drag you down because they tend to not make you feel good after you spend time with them.

In the spiritual world, the word "vibration" gets thrown around a lot. It simply refers to the energy you are giving off. Everything is made up of energy. As the first law of thermodynamics states, "Energy is neither created nor destroyed." It simply changes from one frequency to the next. Think for a moment about your own energy.

You have to match your vibration to how you want to feel. Ever heard of the saying, "Your vibe attracts your tribe?" Well, it's true. The energy you emit attracts like energy. If you are down in the dumps and hating life, bad things are more likely to come your way. But if you choose to raise your vibration, the universe will respond to that by bringing similar energy to you.

The quickest, most fun way I raise my vibration is by having a dance party! I love to turn up some of my favorite music and let my body move. Most of the time, my kids jump in, and soon, we are all dancing around! It just makes you feel good to dance; it gets your blood pumping, and it always seems to put you in a good mood.

By moving around, we are getting rid of the stagnate energy within our bodies that is weighing us down. This is why working out makes you feel better or why runners are always talking about the "runner's high." Regular movement releases old energy and creates a higher vibratory frequency.

If you're not a dancer, watch a stand-up comedy special on Netflix, take a walk in nature, or belt out your favorite tunes while you're driving. Do something that puts a smile on your face. Whatever it is will surely raise your energy level and vibration.

Now, some people are more aware of their surrounding energy than others, and those people are often called empaths, or highly sensitive people. Empaths can very easily walk into a room and pick up on the vibrations or moods of others. I've been an empath all my life but didn't realize it until my early twenties when psychologists started writing about it. Empaths can sense other people's feelings and emotions without talking to them; they simply pick up on those energetic vibrations.

Empaths have to take extra care to protect themselves from other people's energy so they don't take on that person's feelings as their own. It can be a real downer when you are feeling good and someone pulls your energy down to match theirs.

So now that you understand a little bit more about energetics, tap into the vibration you want to live in. Think about how it will feel to succeed and strive and try to match that energetic level each and every day.

Focus on how achieving your goals makes you feel and how it raises your vibration.

Here are some rules when it comes to manifesting:

1. Get very clear on what you desire.
2. What do you want to *be*? How will it make you *feel*? What do you want to *have*?
3. Visualize what your life would look like with this thing you desire.

4. Release all doubts and expectations of how these things will play out. It's up to the universe to make them occur if it's in your highest good.

5. *Trust* that the universe will provide.

Reflection Questions:

◊ Where do you see yourself next year? In five years?

◊ What makes you happy?

◊ What do you see yourself jumping out of bed for every morning?

◊ If you could have your dream life, what would that look like? What would you be doing? Where would you be living?

◊ Write down what your perfect day looks like.

Lesson 3

Creating a Sacred Space

Today's Affirmation:

Today is full of endless possibilities.

If we want to incorporate a daily spiritual practice into our lives, we must make space for that to happen within our homes. We all need a place to retreat to, a place where we can sink into reflection or a meditative energy, a place that calms us.

This could be a small corner in your room, a side table, or an entire room dedicated to your practice. It's important to make do with what you have.

I personally invested in a small trunk I found at a secondhand shop and put it in the corner of my bedroom. Inside, I keep all of my oracle decks, candles, seasonal decorations I can switch out when I feel called to, my shamanic drum, and my journals. Everything I need for my daily practice is within an arm's reach.

So, today, your task is to find a corner in your home you can reserve for your daily practice, a place that invites you to meditate. It should be free from distractions, like computers and TVs, somewhere you can create a little altar if you want. Place a picture of your favorite goddess, set out your jar of goals and aspirations, and include a gratitude journal. Add whatever inspires you.

I like to change my space up to represent the seasons, and I love to incorporate the four elements of earth, air, fire, and water into my space as well. It brings earth energy indoors and helps keep me grounded and balanced.

Some ideas to include in your sacred space for each element are:

◊ Earth: Crystals, flowers, salt, plants, and/or flat meditative stones

◊ Air: Bells, feathers, butterflies (or pictures of other animals with wings), a diffuser with your favorite essential oils, a mini speaker to play meditative music, and/or a singing bowl

◊ Fire: Candles and/or allow the sun to shine in on your space

◊ Water: Seashells, chalice, starfish, a bowl filled with water, a cup of water, and/or driftwood

Keep affirmations, mantras, or pictures of icons or loved ones nearby, things that will inspire you. Use this space as a vision board of sorts. It's nice to have daily reminders and visuals of our goals and aspirations.

It's also important to note in this lesson that our homes often reflect our moods and the inner workings of our minds. I've personally found that I get very stressed out when my home starts to become cluttered. By spending some time decluttering and picking up my home, I can feel much better almost immediately.

If I'm feeling lost or confused about a situation, I often take some time to clean my home. I allow myself to get lost in the mindless tasks of mopping or wiping surfaces clean. It is in these moments that I am able to be very present with the task at hand, see my current situation more clearly, or distance myself from it and realize I don't need to get quite so worked up.

I always feel better after cleaning, even if it's just for twenty minutes or so. Plus, I get to reap the benefits of having a clean house (I have three dogs and two kids; it doesn't last long!). I encourage you to not only look around at the current state of your space and see how it reflects your mental landscape, but also carve out a sacred space that is all your own. Everyone should have a place to turn to for quiet reflection.

Reflection Questions:

◊ What practices would you like to include in your daily spiritual practice?

◊ What habits will you implement that encourage spiritual growth?

◊ How does your current home reflect your mental landscape?

Lesson 4

Self-Care for Your Temple Body

Today's Affirmation:

My body is a temple,
and I treat it as such.

We must all come to the understanding that our bodies are sacred temple spaces. We only get one body in this lifetime, and we should treat it with respect. What we put into our bodies is what we will get out of it, just like everything else in life. So it's important we take the time to give our bodies what they need, such as healthy food and exercise.

If we commit to having healthier bodies, we will naturally feel better. I'm not talking about going on a diet because I don't believe in them. Diets are temporary changes that yield temporary results. I'm talking about a lifestyle change.

Make the time in your schedule to go to a yoga class every week, or start by taking a stroll after dinner one evening. Start small.

Take fifteen minutes today (right now!) and do a few pushups and/or sit ups. Put the book down! I'll wait . . .

Acknowledge where you are physically. This can be your starting point. And then, commit to treating your body better. If you smoke, stop. You are putting toxic chemicals into your lungs that get carried throughout your bloodstream.

I used to work in the medical field—for vascular surgeons to be exact—and one day, they let me watch one of their open abdominal-aortic aneurysm repairs. They had to cut a man open, put him on bypass, and take out a section of his aorta (the main blood vessel leading out of your heart that pumps blood to the rest of the body) and replace it with an artificial one. The surgeon turned and showed me the plaque that was clogging the man's arteries after years of smoking and poor diet choices. I will never forget that image of the surgeon's hand full of gunk that he had scraped out of that man's blood vessel.

Seriously, the body you have right now is it. That's all you get. There are no second chances, so treat it as the sacred temple space it is. Your body is what keeps you alive. It allows you to think clearly, breathe the fresh air outdoors, and pump blood to all of your extremities. Heart disease is still the number one cause of death in the U.S., and it's something that is so preventable by eating a healthy diet and getting regular exercise.

If you want, you can start a food journal by writing down everything you eat in one week and reflecting on the choices you made
and how your body felt after eating certain foods. I know, for me
personally, I absolutely loved ice cream. I grew up consuming
dairy like the rest of us, but as I got older, I started to notice how
upset my stomach was every time I ate it. Thankfully, there are
so many milk alternatives now that I don't have to worry, but
I never would have noticed how I felt after consuming dairy if
I hadn't started paying attention to the things I was eating and
how they made me feel.

For those with gluten sensitivities, there are many gluten-free
options available, but I personally love carbs—pasta, bread, piz-
za, you name it—and my body loves it, too, so I keep gluten in my
diet. It's all about making personalized choices. There is so much
noise out there, with advice coming at us from all angles. It's up
to us to decide what is best for us and what isn't. Take a moment
and tune into your own body. Don't try something simply because everyone else is doing it. Diets are fads anyway.

It's important to make healthy choices that will become a part
of your personal lifestyle. Your health is a lifelong commitment;
it's not something you should think about only when you get
sick. Stay on top of your health by visiting your doctor at least
once a year for a checkup. And if MDs aren't your cup of tea, you
can visit a naturopathic doctor, a nurse practitioner, a nutrition-
ist, or a physician assistant. There are a lot of good people out

there who will take the time to educate you about your body and your health.

You have to start making better choices *today* if you want to see different results tomorrow.

You need to make conscious decisions about what you put into your body and consume, including foods, drugs, and alcohol, as well as the products you put on your skin.

Did you know the skin is the largest organ in the body? It easily absorbs all the lotions and creams you apply. Take a second to make sure the products you buy and use don't contain known carcinogens, such as parabens, triclosan, ethanolamines, butyl-hydroxytoluene (BHT), butylated hydroxyanisole (BHA), form-aldehyde, and/or formaldehyde donors.

You can go to ewg.org and pull up their cosmetic database to see if there are any harmful ingredients in the makeup, lotion, and skincare products you use.

It is important we take responsibility for our actions and make informed decisions.

It should go without saying that when we feel better and are taking care of our bodies, we also have more energy, better moods, and improved mental health.

This is the ultimate form of self-love: loving your physical body for where it is on its journey and all it can do. We often take our physical bodies for granted, but it's time to change that. So let this be your sign right here, right now. If you've been wanting to cut back on eating meat, drinking alcohol, or smoking, now is as good of a time as any. And if you've been wanting to join a gym, try a new workout, take up hiking, or eat more vegetables, here is your chance.

While most of this book is about our spiritual bodies, we can't forget about our mental and physical bodies. Take care of the ones you've got.

Reflection Questions:

◊ What is your current relationship with your body like?

◊ Do you currently treat your body as a sacred temple space?

◊ What improvements could you make to honor your body more?

◊ Is there a bad habit you need to get rid of? What is it?

◊ What steps can you take to make better consumption choices?

Lesson 5

Showcasing Your Best Self

Today's Affirmation:

I am beautiful.

I've had two opposing opinions on fashion in my life. In my teenage years and into college, I adored fashion, the runway, and the latest trends. I took up sewing, made my own clothes, and thought I was destined for a life in the fashion industry. My minor in college was merchandising, and I've managed a few retail stores in my day.

As I got older and fast fashion began to take over, I saw the waste that was being produced. I went through a spiritual awakening and decided it didn't matter what I wore because I didn't care what people thought about me; I wasn't trying to impress anyone anymore. I was married and not trying to attract anyone new, so it didn't matter if I lived in yoga pants and put my hair up every day.

Then, I thought about the power that wearing clothes can have on someone. Wearing an outfit that makes you feel beautiful can have a really positive effect on your self-esteem and how you carry yourself. Fashion, whether we want to admit it or not, is a part of our daily lives—we all have to wear clothes—so we need to learn to invest in practical pieces of clothing that are of good quality and bring us joy. What's the point in paying five dollars for a T-shirt if it's going to unravel after a few washes? By investing in our wardrobes, we invest in ourselves.

I've always been in love with Parisian fashion. The looks are simplistic yet put together, effortless and chic, and I love the idea of having a staple wardrobe. I've personally cleaned out my closet quite a bit over the last few years (remember, I used to work in retail and took full advantage of my employee discount) and have shrunk my wardrobe down to staple items that can be mixed and matched. I also divide my clothes up by season and store them away when they're not in use. Every three months feels like Christmas as I unbox the current season's clothes and rediscover my favorite pieces all over again.

Just as we need to make better choices when it comes to our health, we also need to make better consumer choices, and I like to think we are already seeing this shift occurring. There is a reason a lot of stores and retailers have gone bankrupt and closed their doors; no one was shopping there anymore. They weren't selling us the things we wanted, and in addition, we've turned to buying things online. Speaking of, I urge you to really determine if that cheap or free shipping makes an item worth it. Does it truly bring you happiness? Do you really need it?

Switching gears for today, I want you to dress up. I want you to put on clothes that make you feel beautiful. Whether you put on fancy lingerie, a red lipstick you were saving for a fancy occasion, or the expensive, fancy jewelry you keep tucked away, it doesn't matter; I want you to put it on.

Today, you get to adorn yourself. Whatever makes you feel beautiful, powerful, and sensual, do that! Put on the perfume, wear the high heels, spend some extra time doing your hair or makeup. If you can take a nice, long, hot bath and soak before you get yourself ready, even better. Whatever you've been holding on to for a special occasion, wear it! Every day is a special occasion because every day, you get to wake up and live your life!

Today is all about feeling beautiful, even if you woke up in a crummy mood, stressed out, or bloated. Turn your day around and embrace your soft curves, accentuate your cat eyes with some liner, and paint those luscious lips of yours. Spend some extra time pampering yourself as you get ready for the day. Remember, you are beautiful and deserve to feel as such.

Reflection Questions:

◊ What makes you feel beautiful?

◊ How can you dress up today and take your normal routine to the next level?

◊ When the day is done, take some time to reflect back on how that made you feel? Did you act differently? Did it elevate your mood?

◊ How can you incorporate these ideas into your daily routine?

◊ Take note of how your mood shifts based on the specific pieces of clothing you wear.

Lesson 6

Mindset

Today's Affirmation:

I am worthy of love and success.

The mind is a powerful tool. It can talk you out of or into anything at any time, it can help you overcome any difficulties, or even keep you stuck and afraid of change. We have to be conscious of our thoughts and how they shape our actions and lives.

Although our minds are powerful tools, they can get us into a lot of trouble if we let them. We can invent entire scenarios in our heads that have never occurred. We often watch others' body language and try to interpret it a certain way, when maybe the person didn't mean to send that message at all. We can talk ourselves out of anything with self-doubt and a feeling of unworthiness.

If we aren't careful, our minds can inhibit us from living a full life. By learning to harness our thoughts and implement a grateful, more positive attitude, we can retrain ourselves to see the good in any situation.

If you want to be the owner of a six-figure business, you have to think like a boss would. If you want to be the best cyclist/writer/ graphic designer/_____ (insert your dream job here), you have to believe it's a possibility.

Your mind influences how you think about things, how you process information, and how you move forward with that given information. With that in mind, you can create new realities for yourself. You can wake up every morning ready to take on the day and give it your absolute best. You have to tell yourself you have what it takes and that, one day, when you're ready, everything will fall into place. That is faith.

You must put faith into the universe. You must tell it exactly what you want out of this lifetime so it has a chance to respond and forge the path that is in your highest good.

Now, of course, not everything we want will come to pass because some things just aren't meant for us, and that's OK. We have to accept that our life path will unfold exactly how it's meant to. We will make choices that will teach us lessons and allow us to meet the right people at the right time.

You must adopt a mindset that allows you to believe you are worthy of everything good that is coming to you. By working on your mindset each and every day, you will be able to see all the many blessings that come your way. You have to remind yourself that you are worthy of love and success. You are capable of achieving whatever it is you want out of life. Read that again: You are capable of achieving whatever it is you want out of life.

A few years ago, I started a gratitude journal. Each morning, I woke up and listed three things I was grateful for. Sometimes it was simple things, like the hot coffee my husband made for me in the morning before he went to work, and other times, it was a great conversation I had with a friend or client. On the days I had trouble thinking of something to write, I remembered the basic life necessities I so often took for granted, like the food in my stomach, the clothes on my back, or the roof over my head.

Since I began expressing gratitude every morning, I'm better able to recognize just how many little blessings I have in my life. It's when we are truly grateful that the universe delivers more to us. Gratitude attracts abundance. It's all about the energy you give off. What you put out into the universe will come back to you.

I learned this the hard way one year. My husband and I were struggling financially, our kids were very young, and both of our cars broke down in the middle of the summer. We spent weeks taking our car back and forth to the repair shop, but we eventually had to cave in and purchase a new vehicle and add to our ever-increasing debt with a car loan. That summer, I kept laughing to myself, thinking there was nothing in the world that could possibly make our situation worse, but I got what I asked for. Soon after, things around our house began breaking, and we had to borrow even more money for other things we couldn't afford to fix. Looking back, it was my mindset that brought on those disasters.

And sure, you might be thinking, "But bad things happen all the time; people don't ask for that." But it was my attitude about the entire situation; I was so stressed out, unhappy, and afraid of what might happen next that my energetic vibration attracted the next bad thing to happen.

I've been on both ends of this experiment. I've been so in flow with my work and constantly expressing gratitude that money started coming to me easily. In those moments, I was in alignment with positive vibrations.

Think about a time when you've complained about someone or something. How did it feel in your body? Probably not too good. That kind of energy pulls you down, and you end up moping about for some time afterward because you can't get it out of your head.

Now, think about a time when you were ecstatic and overcome with joy. How did *that* feel in your body? You were most likely energized, with adrenaline coursing through your veins. You probably felt like you were on top of the world. It's a much different energy than complaining or feeling down about something.

It all starts with your mindset. It's a perspective shift. You have to start with your mind if you want to be happy. You have to tell yourself you deserve to be happy, that good things surround you, and a change is just around the corner.

By changing my mindset, I was able to overcome depression twice in my life—once when I was a teenager and again in my mid-twenties. During my more recent depressive episode, I thought there was no point in living, that my friends and family were better off without me. These were things I told myself on a regular basis. I didn't find joy in my day-to-day life. I thought everything had fallen apart, and I couldn't see a way out.

Slowly, though, I started to realize my inner dialogue was preventing me from seeing the light at the end of the tunnel. I decided to change my mindset, and instead of telling myself it would be easier if I died, I told myself my situation was temporary. I told myself that, in a month or a year from now, things were going to look different.

While my mindset could have easily been to blame for my depressive state, it was also the thing that saved me. It pulled me out of the hazy slumber I had self-induced. And now, every time I go through a difficult phase, I remind myself that it is all temporary—every moment, every situation, every conversation. Nothing lasts forever. You can easily find yourself in a new situation or new location in a week.

So if you are reading this and are currently dealing with something extremely difficult, remind yourself that this too shall pass. This situation is temporary. It can all change, but you have to be willing to let it change as well. You have to believe it will get better. You have to believe you deserve better.

Take some time today to remind yourself of all the great things that are already going on in your life instead of focusing your attention and energy on the bad.

Recognize the role your self-dialogue plays in how you perceive things to be versus how they really are.

Reflection Questions:

◊ What are you grateful for right now in your life? List fifty to one hundred things that give you a reason to smile.

◊ How has your inner dialogue affected your mood?

◊ Do you speak kindly to yourself? If not, how can you switch your mindset to be more encouraging and forgiving?

Lesson 7

Letting Go

Today's Affirmation:

I release all that no longer serves me.

Letting go can be a hard thing to do sometimes. We often hold on to things hoping they might change, or we remember the times someone wronged us just so we can keep score for a later date. We use it as leverage, and we hold grudges. We have a hard time moving past the trauma that was inflicted upon us.

We often hold on to certain ideas that are antiquated, having a hard time believing something else could be true, or we hold on to the idea that we aren't worthy of success, that we don't belong in a particular place, or we aren't good enough for a certain job.

Sometimes we need to let go of the things that are hindering our growth and ability to move on.

Some of these hinderances include:

◊ Old, unhealthy habits

◊ Perfectionism

◊ Limiting beliefs

◊ Societal expectations (e.g. Being the "good girl")

◊ Victim mentality where we think things happen *to* us

◊ Old friends or past relationships that no longer serve us

◊ Self-sabotage

◊ Self-doubt

You need to let go of the belief that you are not worthy or are incapable of change. Let go of the fear of what might happen if you did let go. Start thinking about all the positive things that *could* happen once you do let go. Our souls usually put us through cycles until we learn our lesson, grow, and move on.

Think about the same boring, unfulfilling jobs you've taken or the relationships you've had with partners who never treated you right or the same fight you have with your partner time and time again because you've never come to an agreement. Something needs to change for these cycles to stop occurring. Usually this means letting go of fear, limiting beliefs, or societal expectations. We have to walk a new path and make a different decision than we have before. And in some cases, we have to walk away from a relationship or physically move altogether.

We tend to fight tooth and nail to stay in these toxic scenarios because we don't want to change. We tell ourselves that change is scary and it takes too much effort to fight all the time, so we learn to accept our current circumstances, daydreaming of the day when our problems will be solved for us.

But the truth is if we can let go of those circumstances and consciously choose to move forward, we usually find ourselves looking back thinking, *What the hell was I thinking?*

In another instance, it can be our comparisons to others' experiences that holds us back; when we don't get the same results as someone else, we get upset. But when we surrender to what the universe is trying to guide us toward, we often realize we were on the wrong path all along.

Take, for example, one of my beautiful friends I went on a women's retreat with. We spent the day opening up to different archetypes of the divine feminine, some more potent than others. There was one in particular she had a hard time energetically opening up to. Women all around her were crying or on their knees, having these big emotional reactions, and she was stuck. Afterward, she got upset with herself because she wasn't experiencing it like the rest of the women, but in that moment, she wasn't ready to open up to that energy.

It's easy for me to say you have to be quiet and let your intuition guide you, but you might have a much harder time connecting with that part of yourself than others. And that's OK. Your experience is OK. Sometimes we subconsciously block ourselves out of fear of what will come up or be revealed to us. We ignore things and pretend they aren't there because we don't want to deal with them.

But there is an art and beauty in surrendering to the moment, in accepting what is to move forward. If something isn't working out in your life right now, perhaps it's not meant to be in your life.

For years, I thought I wanted to go to nursing school. Even after I graduated college and had a bachelor's degree, I went back and completed all of my credits to apply to nursing school, and the day I went to turn in my application, they told me I wouldn't be able to because I was missing one grade. It was a class I had already completed online, but they weren't going to be posting my grade for another seven days.

I missed applying to nursing school by seven days. And when the deadline came around the following year, I still wanted to apply, but I became pregnant with my first child and did not want to be in school while becoming a brand new mother. Nursing school wasn't in the cards for me. And while I still found jobs in the medical field and could have chosen to go back after my kids were born, I found that I truly didn't want it. Even though it was something I pursued for years, taking countless additional courses, I knew deep down that wasn't my path or my calling.

I had to surrender and let go of the idea that I would be a nurse. It simply wasn't in the cards for me. And I'm sure you, too, have tried something in your life, but the timing was off. It's in those moments we can learn to surrender and let the dream go. We can simply give our control to the situation and allow what is meant to happen to unfold.

We often try so hard to control things that are, in reality, out of our control. I know I did for the longest time. Having control in certain situations gave me a sense of security and purpose. It made me feel organized in a time of chaos. It gave me structure. But what I ended up realizing is that it didn't really give me the freedom I thought I had. It was an illusion.

When I had a newborn baby and became a mother for the first time, I read all the parenting and birthing books I could and thought I was ready to give birth to my baby. But when my water broke, the birth center already had two other moms in labor; nothing went according to plan.

Motherhood taught me to relinquish a lot of my control. My son never napped when I wanted him to, and my daughter refused to take a bottle and exclusively breastfed; those little infants wouldn't give in. As toddlers, they have minds of their own, and

I learned very quickly that I couldn't control them. My daughter is fiercely independent with a mind of her own (much like her mama), and there is no telling her what to do.

So, I threw up my hands and surrendered to parenthood. I learned to surrender to my children (in certain situations, not all) so they can learn through their own mistakes. It doesn't matter how many times you tell them to hold the cup with two hands so they don't spill their drink. Sometimes you just have to let them spill it to see for themselves, and then you teach them how to clean it up.

Life always takes us through cycles of death and rebirth. What do you need to let go of to make room for growth? What endings need to occur for new things to emerge?

This might take some time to figure out. The answer might not come to you right away. But spend the day thinking of what no longer serves you.

There is beauty in surrendering; letting go is an art form. So often in our lives, we push and push until we get what we *think* we want. When things don't go our way, we try different routes to get where we want to go. But what we don't learn while growing up is that instead of pushing our way into something, we also have a choice to simply surrender.

Reflection Questions:

◊ What is holding you back from stepping into your full authentic self?

◊ What is limiting you from the life you want?

◊ What restraints might you be putting on yourself?

◊ What do you need to let go of to move forward?

Lesson 8

Accessing Shakti

Today's Affirmation:

I am part of the divine,
and the divine is a part of me.

Shakti is a goddess in the Hindu pantheon who represents the feminine generative power. When we speak about Shakti, we are talking about the feminine life force energy that moves freely within us all. It's uncontrollable, unpredictable, raw power. It ebbs and flows. It is the unconscious.

Shiva is the masculine, the anchor, the container. It symbolizes consciousness. Shiva and Shakti make up two parts of a whole. We cannot have masculine without feminine, just as we are all composed of both masculine and feminine energies and traits.

The best explanation I've heard for Shiva and Shakti is from Sabrina Domenosky's *Rewilding for Women* podcast. She explained that Shiva is the atmosphere, while Shakti is the weather.

The masculine holds the space, and within that space, the feminine dances and moves wildly. The weather can be sunny and beautiful, ferocious and deadly, or like a soft rain shower. Just as with the feminine, there are many emotions, and the masculine is in a steady constant, acting as a container.

The masculine and feminine naturally complement each other, but we are raised in a world where primarily embodying your masculine energy is praised. The masculine is action-oriented and gets things done, while the feminine is much more passive, letting things flow as they come about.

The masculine is strong, protective, and unyielding, while the feminine is soft, nurturing, and open. The feminine has a different sort of strength; it's not about physical strength as much as it is about inner strength and finding the willpower and perseverance to carry on. Of course, if you've ever seen a mama bear protect her cubs, you know she, too, can be fierce and protective.

Unfortunately, young girls aren't really encouraged to get to know their bodies as they grow up, causing them to become disconnected from them as adults. If this sounds like you, you're in luck because, today, we are going to practice accessing our inner Shakti. I urge you to open up to the feminine part of yourself, the soft and sensual side.

Shakti energy often resides in the sacral chakra, which is a lower chakra point residing at the base of your spine. There is a lot of creative energy that lies within our wombs, which we will cover in another lesson. The best way to open up to this energy is to move your body.

Find some instrumental shamanic music, either through a simple search on YouTube or by googling "Shakti" or "kundalini" music.

Kundalini is a Sanskrit term meaning "to experience the rising of energy and consciousness." It's what occurs when we have an awakening. Kundalini is also thought to be located at the base of the spine.

By moving our bodies to music, we are able to loosen ourselves up, which, in turn, opens up our energetic portals. Shakti is thought to be serpentine energy. The snake is very much a feminine symbol, as the Christians long associated it with the Garden of Eden and Eve's "sin" of falling for temptation.

Today, find some time to move your body; dance and tune in to how your body wants to move. Awaken the snake within you, dear sister. Let the creative life force energy inside of you arise, surround, and engulf you. Let yourself get lost in your dance.

Don't worry about what you look like doing this. Close the door to your bedroom or go to a place where you can be alone, close your eyes, and start to sway. Pay attention to how you feel. Pay attention to your body and the signals it sends you.

For some women, dancing might be an easy, fun task, but others might be self-conscious of their dance moves. Whether you can dance or not does not matter. Just start with your feet planted firmly on the ground and rock your hips back and forth. That motion alone is enough to awaken the Shakti within you.

Reflection Questions:

◊ How was your energy and mood prior to your Shakti dance? How did you feel afterward?

◊ Did you have any new insights?

◊ What emotions came up for you?

◊ How did stepping into this energy make you feel?

Lesson 9

Womb Wisdom

Today's Affirmation:

I am unstoppable.

As women, we have the ability to create and birth new life. Our wombs are amazing powerhouses of creative energy, and as we learned in yesterday's lesson, it holds Shakti energy. But our wombs aren't just made for making babies. This area of our body also inspires us to birth new projects, businesses, stories, art pieces, or whatever else it can think of and put out into the world.

Here are a few awesome facts about your womb. The uterus is the strongest muscle in the body. Typically, your uterus is about the size of your fist, but of course, it can grow significantly in nine months. The uterus is also the only organ that can grow another organ (the placenta) inside it! When you're pregnant, the placenta attaches to the uterine walls and carries nutrients from you to your baby. Menstrual blood also contains an amazing amount of stem cells.

The average menstrual cycle lasts about twenty-nine-and-a-half days, while the average lunar cycle is twenty-eight days. I don't believe this is a coincidence. The moon represents the feminine, while the sun is the masculine. Our menstrual cycles are closely tied to the lunar phases, and just like the moon, we, too, go through phases each month.

During our menstrual cycles, we first bleed, then the follicular phase, ovulation, and the luteal phase follow. During the moon cycle, the moon starts off dark (new moon), then waxes, becomes full, then wanes. The moon affects the tides of the ocean, and since our body is mostly comprised of water, I have no doubt it affects us, too.

Pay attention to the lunar cycles as you ovulate and bleed, for there are two categories you can fall into. If you bleed during the full moon and ovulate during the new moon, this is considered to be the red moon cycle. You are most fertile and creative during the full moon and tend to retreat inward during the new moon. This is the cycle of the creatrix, the woman who tends to put a lot of creative energy out into the world.

Opposite of that is the white moon cycle, where you bleed during the new moon and ovulate during the full moon. Those on the white moon cycle are said to be in their mother phase. They are most intuitive during their menstruation, and they feel the need to retreat during this time, as they have spent the majority of the month taking care of others.

Now, obviously, there are a lot of exceptions to this rule. You might bleed and ovulate somewhere in the middle. You might feel your most creative at another part of the moon cycle. The whole point here is to understand your menstrual cycle and your moods and emotions that ebb and flow during that time.

Take some time to track your cycle and get in tune with it. As children, we are raised to shun our periods. We grow up thinking our periods are a nuisance and we should just put a tampon in and forget out about them when they show up. We think menstrual blood is gross and inconvenient. Many women elect to go a year or longer without their periods if they can. But I want to ask you, why?

How do you feel about your menstrual cycle? Is it a time you dread? Over half of the population is made up of women. That means half of the world bleeds. It's time we embrace our cycles and learn to change our thinking around them. Our periods are a natural part of us, so it's vital that we pay attention to them and learn about our own phases throughout the month and how we can embrace those moments when we feel most creative or need to retreat and relax.

We can learn to build our schedules around our own moon cycles, giving us time to turn inward when needed and be more social when we have more energy. I urge you to track your cycle with the lunar phase for twenty-eight days. Write down how you emotionally feel each day and how your body feels; track it with colors or using a number scale of one to ten—whatever works best for you. After a few months, notice the patterns that show up for you.

I can clearly remember my first period. It didn't come until after my fifteenth birthday, but that first year was unbearable. I had terrible pain and heavy bleeding, and I begged my mother to put me on birth control to stabilize it. I didn't want to deal with it. I ended up staying on birth control for almost ten years. Looking back, I wonder if it would have stabilized on its own if I had given my body a chance.

Not only do our wombs sync up with the natural cycles of Mother Nature, but our wombs also carry wisdom, healing, creative energy, and divine mysteries. You were first conceived inside of a womb. You carry with you the energetic imprint of your mother's womb, as do all of your brothers and sisters. If you have children, they each carry the imprint of your womb as well.

The womb holds a lot of memories and wisdom, as well as trauma. It's a place where we tend to bury our emotions and wounds. If you've been sexually abused, it could be a painful thing to think about, but it's our job to heal those wounds and work through the pain we carry so as not to pass it on to our children.

It's our job as women to prepare younger girls—our daughters, nieces, and granddaughters—for their periods and teach them to honor the time in a girl's life when she becomes a woman. Men used to have ceremonies all the time to celebrate their rites of passage. We should be doing this for our girls as well to help them understand their bodies, prepare them for the changes, and teach them that it isn't something to dread; it's a cause for celebration.

There has been too much shame and stigma surrounding our menstrual cycles and wombs. We seem to only honor women when they are pregnant and having babies. But what about our young girls? What about the older, post-menopausal women who are settling into their crone years? When will we start to honor them as well?

All women have the ability to connect with Mother Nature and create whatever life she desires, and every woman contains the universe's life force energy within her womb space. If you are reading this and no longer have a womb, have no fear! You still have access to the womb space. There doesn't need to be a physical womb for you to access the wisdom, mysteries, and energy of Shakti. We can tap into it at any point in our lives.

It doesn't matter if we find ourselves in the maiden, mother, or crone stage of our lives; we are all able to benefit and feel the life force energy residing within us.

Meditating on your womb space helps you open the doors to the mysteries of the divine feminine. Imagine yourself deep within your womb space. What do you feel? What arises? What are you holding on to in your womb that needs to be released? What wants to be birthed?

Take a few moments and put a hand on your womb space and breath into it. Sink in as deeply as you can. Having the physical touch of your hand might help you focus on that area. You might need to sway or rock your hips to awaken the space. Maybe you need to rub or tap that area with your hands. Do whatever helps you draw attention to your womb, then allow yourself to surrender. Deepen this space. Don't question what comes up for you, just let it flow through you. Let any emotions that need to arise flow out of you. This is the wisdom of the womb. This is where our creative energy comes from.

Reflection Questions:

◊ Are you on the red or white moon cycle or somewhere in between?

◊ What was your relationship like with your womb prior to today's lesson?

◊ How do you feel about your moon cycle now?

◊ Do you have any past trauma or pain that you need to confront?

◊ If you no longer have a physical womb, what emotions arise when you think of your energetic womb space?

◊ What are you looking to birth into the world?

Lesson 10

Embodiment

Today's Affirmation:

I embody love, light, and truth.

I want to introduce you to a new way of looking at things. Instead of perceiving things with your mind, constantly trying to rationalize everything and make sense of it, what if you turned inward to your body? What if you decided to embody how you were feeling? What if you used your body to help you make decisions and feel your way through situations?

I'm the first person to admit I can easily overanalyze everything. I'm a recovering perfectionist, after all. But when I started to include embodiment practices into my daily routine, things became a lot less stressful, and I had less frequent headaches.

Embodiment is simply tuning into your body and letting it move freely. The best and quickest way I've found to get out of my head and into my body is through dance, as I've mentioned before.

Embodiment practices can also include yoga, martial arts, gardening, working on your posture, or working with your hands.

When we choose to quiet our thoughts and let our bodies do the talking, we quickly realize we can be engulfed in certain feelings.

Take, for example, pleasure. When you embody pleasure and let it arise naturally, it seems to radiate throughout your entire being. Your body starts to tingle, a smile comes across your lips, and you sink into the feeling, letting it pull you into a state of bliss.

Well, you can easily tap into those feelings once more when you start practicing embodiment, when you realize you are a vessel of love, joy, and light. You can tap into that frequency by simply moving your body to the tune of that vibration.

We are not meant to be sedentary creatures. We are meant to play, explore, and stretch ourselves and our limits to see just how far we can go. We are meant to make love and art and use our hands.

The next time it rains, step outside and feel the cool drops on your skin, or when you are in your garden, notice how the soil feels when you start digging with your bare hands. The next time you paint, try using your hands instead of a brush. Notice the different textures you touch throughout your day. Pay more attention to what surrounds you and how your body interacts with it. This is just a small practice to get you out of your head and more in tune with your body.

This may be challenging at first because it is not something we are ever taught to think about, but when we start to practice embodiment, we can easily turn our attention back into our bodies whenever we are feeling stressed or anxious. We can start to move our bodies and allow that negative energy to be released.

This also comes in handy when we start to uncover feminine archetypes, which we will talk about more in Lesson 20. With embodiment, we can start to tap into the frequency of an archetype and embody whichever one we are feeling called to in the moment.

As a quick example, picture yourself as a queen sitting on your throne with a crown on your head. When you start to imagine yourself in this way, does your posture straighten? Do you hold your chin up a little bit higher? Does a sense of power and sovereignty rise up within you?

If you answered yes to any of those questions, it's because you just embodied the archetype of a queen. Some days, this archetype can help us out when we aren't feeling confident or can't picture ourselves as a leader.

Today, take some time to stand still in your room and sway back and forth. How does your body want to move? Do your arms want to dance beside you? Without music, drop into your body and notice the sensations that arise. Notice how your sways might turn into circles or pick up the tempo.

When your mind starts to relax, pick a feeling you want to embody. Perhaps you want to embody joy or pleasure. Think about how those feel in your body. What sensations start to arise? Notice if you get chills or goosebumps or if your heart starts to swell. Embody the feeling you want to experience. This is all about getting out of your head and into your body.

Reflection Questions:

◊ What type of embodiment practice can you incorporate into your day today?

◊ What feelings do you want to embody? How does that feeling differ from how you are currently feeling? How can you close the gap between the two?

◊ In what ways is your body asking to be moved?

Lesson 11

Developing Your Intuition

Today's Affirmation:

Everything I'm looking for
I can find within me.

Ilike to think of intuition as your inner compass, that part of you that knows things without knowing how or why you know them. It's the part of yourself you should turn to when you feel confused or unsure of a situation.

We often discredit our intuition. Our mind prefers logic, which makes us believe we have to have an explanation for everything. But this is not how we are meant to live all the time. There are times in our lives where logic cannot help us, and we must rely on our intuition, our inner knowing, to make the best decisions for ourselves.

Intuition has guided me my entire life. As a little girl, I always felt I was following my heart, and in a way, I was. I did what made me happy. I was being guided by my inner knowing.

I've relied on my intuition for all the decisions I've made in my life up until I was about twenty years old. Things changed after I graduated college, though; I started listening to all the adults in my life, the people who were cut off from their own inner knowing. I thought I had to get a job; I thought I just needed a paycheck. I wasn't *supposed* to like what I was doing, but I needed to support myself.

I felt like the life was being sucked out of me. You might think I was the girl who didn't want to grow up, but that's not the case at all. As a young girl, I dreamed of being an adult, driving a car, and having responsibilities and independence. I wanted the freedom to make my own decisions and mistakes and learn my own way.

It was when I started to blend into the cultural norm that I felt I lost my way. I started to suppress what made me happy. I did as I was told and became the adult that got up, went to work, came home, drank a lot to forget about my miserable day, went to bed, and got up the next day to repeat the same cycle. Day in and day out, my life was passing me by.

I forgot about passion. I ignored all of those little bread crumbs that would have led me out of those situations. You know those sparks of insight and creativity, those ideas that light a fire within you? Those are intuitive hits.

As adults, we make *so many* excuses as to why we don't follow those sparks. We say, "I don't have time to paint; I'm too old to start a dance class; I never have time to write or be creative."

But think about this: Maybe those sparks of joy, those intuitive hits, could lead you to a new, better life. What if we started to listen to our inner compass more? What if we actually made time in our day or week to do the things we enjoy, whether it's learning a new skill or language or traveling the world?

Paying attention to my intuition has saved me from a lot of trouble. I've left jobs that were soul-sucking. I've left relationships that weren't mutual or made me feel disrespected. I even moved across the country at the age of eighteen to live on my own for the first time, which was the scariest yet most rewarding experience of my life.

That year, I learned more life lessons than I would have in a decade if I had not moved; I'm sure of it. Granted, I didn't understand them at the time, but that year of my life was a real struggle. Looking back on it now, I know I wouldn't be where I am today or who I am today if I had not gone through a lot of those things.

Life really is about making mistakes and learning from them. We are always on a journey to grow and expand, yet so many of us settle, suppressing our intuition and not following the sparks we get. So, I ask you, when it comes to those dreams you have of starting a business, moving to a new country, or whatever it is you keep saying "someday" about, what's stopping you from living that dream right here and now?

I know, for me, when I had a job I absolutely abhorred, I would sometimes cry on the way to work. I dreaded going into work, and everything in my body fought going to that place. But of course, my logical, rational mind would tell me, *Courtney, it's a paycheck. It's only for a few hours each day; you can do anything.* I would have to talk myself into going to work. That's when I knew I needed to leave and find something different. No one should ignore feelings as extreme as those. We have them for a reason, but oftentimes, we find it easier to ignore them and go about our daily lives. By quieting our minds and surrendering to the quiet, we are able to strengthen our intuition.

We all feel our intuition in different places in our body. For most people, it's that age-old "gut feeling" you get when something seems off. That gut feeling is located in your sacral chakra, just below your belly button. Or you may get "butterflies" in the pit of your stomach, which means your intuition most likely resides in your solar plexus, or your abdomen. For others, their intuition resides in their heart.

Regardless of where it's located, our intuition is our built-in compass. It's our personalized guidance system. So why don't you spend more time listening to it?

It's so easy to get swept up in the day-to-day grind and stay in our heads rather than in our bodies. The thing is our world is so chaotic, telling us what to buy, how to look, and so on, that we forget about the little voice inside. As a child, we often listened to the guidance and advice of the adults in our lives to make sense of the world around us. But unfortunately, as we became adults ourselves, we didn't stop taking others' advice. Instead, we began seeking it out even more, which smothered our intuition.

It takes practice to tune out the external world and turn inward. But once you develop this skill, you'll notice your intuition becomes louder. You'll be able to easily tune into it and listen to the guidance it's giving you.

Listening to our intuition requires us to have a change of perspective. It requires us to realize that perhaps all the external feelings and emotions we feel aren't really our own but, rather, ones we've picked up from others. It takes practice and a new perspective to discern what is your truth and what is from someone else.

Take a moment today to sit still with your eyes closed. Take a few deep breaths in and out, clear your mind, and ask yourself, "What is my dream? Is there anything in my life I want to change right now in this moment?"

What's the first thing that pops into your head? What is that dream? What do you want to do? What do you want to change? Whatever it is, go with it. Let it unfold in front of you. Let your mind wander. This is your intuition. This is your inner knowing trying to guide you.

If you are drawing a complete blank, try a simpler test to practice tapping into your intuition. The next time you go out to eat or are deciding what to eat for your next meal, give yourself two options. Relax for a moment and think about each option individually. Tune in and see how your body responds to them. Perhaps you're deciding between a salad or chicken noodle soup. Is your body craving more vegetables and a lighter option, or are you wanting comfort food, something to warm you up?

It might sound silly, but our bodies respond to so many things a day. Intuition can be subtle, which is why it's often so overlooked. If you want to continue to develop your intuition, turn to it whenever you have a decision to make. Feel how your body responds.

Reflection Questions:

◊ Do you consider yourself intuitive?

◊ Did you find it easy to quiet your mind and tap into your intuition?

◊ How can you begin making more intuitive decisions in your day-to-day life?

Lesson 12

Unleashing Creativity

Today's Affirmation:

I am full of creative ideas
waiting to be released.

One thing I came across on my own spiritual awakening was my passion for painting and writing (granted, I knew I always wanted to be a writer). I was often told I was creative growing up, but I never truly believed it because I thought my work wasn't as good as other artists I admired.

I hadn't learned that being creative is not about being good or bad. I was still holding on to my inner critic and the idea that everything had to be perfect.

I started to paint to connect with my inner self, to express whatever was inside of me and let it flow out into the world. I came across a woman by the name of Whitney Freya and her book *Rise Above: One Brush Stroke at a Time*. Without ever taking a professional painting class, she opened up her own art studio and started teaching painting.

She helped me realize I didn't need to let anyone else see my work. I could paint just to paint. I started creating for my eyes only. If I was having a bad day, I'd turn on some music, grab a canvas and some paint, and let my emotions pour out of me.

Allowing yourself to surrender and simply create is extremely therapeutic. Surrendering allows us to connect more with ourselves and the divine as well. When you start to create, you get into this zone where all you are focusing on is the project in front of you. You are able to tune out the rest of the world and be present. You can sculpt, write, paint, or draw—whatever it is you are feeling or want to express. Creating allows you to slip into a place where the world, your worries, the drama, and the stress all melt away and disappear.

It's in this state of mind that we are able to open ourselves up to the higher realms, to the possibilities that surround us. We are able to tap into parts of ourselves we might have not known were there.

Being creative has lots of benefits. Working in a creative state liberates us from the need to be perfect. It relieves stress, puts us in a meditative state, and allows us to connect with and access our intuition while giving us a sense of freedom.

The objective for today is to carve out some time to be creative. This might be drawing, coloring, painting, scrapbooking, dancing, or free-writing. What do you want to birth into existence? What emotions need to be released from your mind and body?

When you are in your creative mode, try to release all judgements about yourself and what you are creating. This isn't going in the Guggenheim; it's just an exercise for you. It's to see what you have been holding on to. What signs, symbols, or patterns are you noticing? Let go of the need for perfection. Just let it be. Accept whatever comes out.

Reflection Questions:

◊ How was the creative process for you?

◊ What medium/tools did you choose to use?

◊ What insights did you get during this process?

◊ What signs/symbols/patterns came up?

◊ What is your interpretation of those signs?

Lesson 13

Soul vs. Ego

Today's Affirmation:

I am only responsible for my thoughts
and actions, not anyone else's.

Our egos are our conscious mind, our reality. Our soul is our subconscious, our inner wisdom. It's important to distinguish the two from one another and recognize when our egos are getting in the way of living our soul's truth.

This lesson is about how to determine the difference between the ego and the soul. It takes practice to determine when our egos are talking and how to tune them out. We have to learn how to get out of our own way.

Since our ego is the conscious mind, it governs the realistic part of ourselves. It's the part of the brain that most people turn to the majority of the time. In most cases, the ego can stop us from pursuing our soul's purpose. It's what squanders our intuition.

We have to learn to recognize when we are operating from a place that serves our ego so we can set it aside and allow our soul to speak.

When our soul is turned on, we can start to see signs, symbols, or patterns, such as repeating numbers on the clock or when we think about a person and suddenly get a call or text from them. These are signs from the universe telling you to follow this path. It's trying to give you a message or confirm you are operating from a soul-aligned place.

The ego is self-serving and is based on survival instincts. It is constantly looking out for number one, and likes to place blame on others rather than accept fault. It can hold on to resentment, engage in gossip, and place us in a victim mentality. The ego wants to put up defense mechanisms and is responsible for building walls to keep others away. It can easily justify anger against others, and it loves to compare itself to others.

The ego is also responsible for helping us talk ourselves out of following our dreams and powers. The ego wants to hide; it's afraid to take risks. It wants to keep us small so we can stay safe and not draw unwanted attention to ourselves. But when we let the ego lead and make all of our decisions, we often find ourselves stuck in the same repeating patterns.

Perhaps you wanted to open up your own bakery or boutique, but you keep finding yourself putting it off. Ask yourself why?

Why do I keep putting this off? Am I afraid? If so, what am I afraid of?

You might think you are afraid of failure, afraid that no one will come to your shop, or maybe you are afraid of what your friends and family might think of you. But that's all your ego talking. So what if you fail? You might think you don't know the first thing about running a business, and you might not. Go out and start reading some books about how to start a business or network with other small business owners.

Failure is what helps us grow. We have to try and try again if we want to be good at anything. This is why athletes practice almost every day; if you want to be the best at something, you have to practice. If you want to run a business and be successful, you have to learn through trial and error. Very rarely does someone succeed on their first try. Ask any entrepreneur, and I guarantee they have a long list of things they tried before finding the one thing that worked.

On the other hand, the soul takes responsibility and ownership of what is happening. It accepts and forgives and is divinely aligned. The soul is able to recognize when others are suffering and are directing their negative energy toward us. The soul can easily forgive; it doesn't allow others' energies to affect its own. The soul is fearless, unafraid of exploring the unknown. It trusts it will be guided and that things will fall into place when it's time.

Take time today to recognize when your ego is trying to control a situation and ask it very lovingly and gently to step aside. Then, start asking for signs from the Divine to guide you towards the right path, and keep an eye out for them!

Reflection Questions:

◊ In what areas of your life are you acting from an ego-based place?

◊ How would your soul react differently?

◊ Do you often find yourself placing blame on others or projecting your problems on to them? In what ways can you correct these tendencies?

Lesson 14

Love Letter

Today's Affirmation:

I am brave, bold, and beautiful.

Today's lesson is very simple. Take some time to write yourself a love letter. Write down all the beautiful and wonderful gifts you possess. Remind yourself of all the trials and tribulations you've gone through and overcome. Remember all those times you struggled but persevered. You are a strong individual who is capable of overcoming anything that is thrown your way.

Write down everything you love about yourself—your sensitivity, uniqueness, inner weirdo, that undying love you have for your cat. It doesn't matter what you include. All that matters is that you recognize what an amazing human being you are. You are needed on this planet right now with everything you have to offer. You might not think you will ever amount to much, but that isn't true, my love.

You are needed. You are loved. So write yourself a love letter. Fall back in love with yourself and everything you have to offer. And on those days when you are feeling down, like you can't push on, like you've been beaten down yet again and can't see a way out, pull out this love letter. Remind yourself of all the struggles you've already overcome. Remind yourself of your talents and strength.

Keep this love letter in your nightstand drawer, tucked inside your planner, or inside your wallet. Have it handy whenever you need a reminder of how wonderful you are. Read through it and feel yourself fill up with love. Because that's what you are. You are love, my darling. You are worthy and capable of giving and receiving love from yourself, the most important person in your world.

It's OK to take care of yourself first. In fact, you have to love yourself first; then and only then can you give love to other people. If you don't love yourself, you will have an empty reservoir.

Have you ever heard the expression "Fill your cup first and give to others with the overflow?" You must fill your cup first with self-love. Once you do that, you can allow others to love you and give love in return. As women, we often get so lost in constantly giving to others that we forget to take care for ourselves. I know I so easily fell into this trap when I was a new mother. I had two babies under the age of two and completely neglected my needs.

It took a breakdown and several therapy sessions to realize I needed to fill my own cup first.

Let me spare you the therapy trips (unless, of course, you want to go, then by all means, therapy is a great tool for self-healing and growth) and tell you that self-care is *not* selfish! I hate to be the bearer of bad news, but no one is going to look out for you except you.

Real talk for a minute, I used to project all of my issues onto my husband, thinking he was going to come to my rescue and fix everything for me, but the truth was he couldn't. He didn't live inside my head. He didn't know the internal dialogue I struggled with.

In truth, my biggest fear used to be that he would cheat on me and leave me for someone else. But I realized I was projecting my own issues of low self-esteem onto him. I thought I wasn't good enough for him, so I worried he would leave me. Hello, wake-up call!

It was only when I started to love myself more and take care of myself that I realized how much I loved my life and my husband. Those were moments of insecurity. I had to relearn to put myself first. I had to give myself love, let my cup overflow, and then I could shower those I loved with my unconditional love.

I hope you find a way to shower yourself in this unconditional love. Previous generations grew up thinking it was rude to talk about themselves and put themselves first. But now, the culture is slowly shifting, and we are recognizing we have to look out for number one, and in part, that's the ego's job. But we have to learn to come from a place of divine love. Love ourselves without condition.

Write your letter and take some time after reading this to take care of you. Soak in the bathtub, buy yourself a drink, curl up and read a book. Do whatever makes you feel good, something you enjoy that you don't spend enough time doing. Stop making excuses as to why you can't and make the time. Time is something we don't get back, so schedule some time for self-care every week. It can be as simple as ten minutes a day or a monthly massage. Schedule it now to avoid burnout in the future. Fill your cup.

Reflection Questions:

◊ What messages will you include in your love letter? What parts of yourself do you love the most? What are some of your greatest achievements?

◊ How can you make more time for self-care and self-love practices?

◊ Are you putting yourself first?

Lesson 15

Unlearning and Rewilding

Today's Affirmation:

I consciously create my future.

Rewilding is a term that has been popping up frequently over the last few years. It's a movement about getting back to nature, but it's also a way to come back home to our soul selves because we are nature, and nature is us. For too long, we have neglected the Mother in our society. We have stripped away her resources, profited off of them, and poisoned her air and rivers.

I remember visiting my granny during the summers as a little girl, spending the days sitting around her table, helping her can fresh vegetables from her garden for the winter. Her nephew would bring corn from his farm, and we would shuck it outside on the patio. The long summer nights would be spent outdoors, running around the yard.

When I was younger, things were definitely simpler, so it's no co-incidence that the minimalism and rewilding movements have sprung up in the last ten years. We are recognizing that we have too much stuff and do too many things, and we are looking for ways to simplify our lives again. We are finding ways to get back to nature.

While technology has enabled us to connect with people from all over the world, it has also isolated us in a way that wasn't possible before. There are several different ways to communicate now. I have so many social media accounts, it gets overwhelming at times.

We've come to a point in the collective where we need to unlearn a lot of things we were brought up to believe, things that no longer ring true for us.

One common example of this is the idea of the "good girl," the idea that women have to behave, hold our tongues, and not cause a scene, the idea that women could be "hysterical." The good girl had to adhere to a certain image; she couldn't dress in provocative clothing or show too much skin because she would attract the wrong attention.

Another example is the idea that success is supposed to look the same for everyone. I grew up believing I had to go to college, and once I graduated, I would find a good-paying job. Somehow having a college degree equaled success, but I graduated in the middle of a recession, and that was not the case for me. I struggled to find a good-paying job after I graduated, and that forced me to learn that success looks different for different people. My version of success looked different from my mother's idea of success. Success is what you make it. It's yours to define alone for yourself. What does your version of success look like? For you, in this moment, what do you aspire to do or be? Without comparing yourself to other people in your field, what is success to you?

We have to unlearn this habit of comparison. As Theodore Roosevelt said, "Comparison is the thief of joy," and it truly is. Comparison robs us of feeling worthy. We think we don't measure up to what others are doing. But the truth is we are all on our own path. Your path is not the same as mine or another person reading this book. We all have different pasts, different personalities, and different skills and gifts. It's so important to unlearn this habit of comparison.

We often look for advice and guidance outside of ourselves. We turn to other people to help us make decisions about our life when, in truth, we should be turning to ourselves, turning inward to our souls to see what rings true for us. Use those intuitive gifts to see which path feels right to you. Ultimately, every decision you make is up to you. You might be in a situation where you don't see a way out or around something you don't want to do, but you always have the choice to walk away. You can always let go or walk away from anything that doesn't feel right to you.

You have the control and power to live up to your soul's purpose. You have an inner guide within you that can give you all the answers you seek.

So why do we turn to others so often? Sometimes we just want someone to listen, and we don't really need or want their opinion or advice. But next time you find yourself asking someone for advice, take a moment and find some silence. Turn your attention inward and ask yourself the same question. What's the first thing that pops up in response to your question? That is your higher self trying to guide you. The more you practice this, the easier it becomes to listen to, the louder it will speak, and the more signs and messages you will notice throughout your day. We learn to pay attention to these things when we turn our attention inward to our higher self.

Another lesson we need to unlearn is the idea of keeping ourselves small. We often think we need to blend in so we don't attract attention to ourselves or intimidate other people. I found this to be true when I went into the workforce. In my early twenties, I landed a job that I was not exactly qualified for, but I put my all into it and learned everything I could about my new chosen field. I was determined to not let my bosses down, and in the process, I think I pissed off some people by making them look bad when they didn't get their work done in the same timeframe. But that's just a part of my personality. I like to excel and do my best by nature. It's also a part of my recovering perfectionist attitude. I intimidated a lot of people in the process, so I slowly learned to keep my mouth shut and lay low. But that really didn't do me any favors; I hid my light in fear of upsetting others.

You don't have to dim your light because you are afraid of shining too brightly. Get over the idea that you have to remain small so you don't rock the boat. The world needs more change-makers and culture-shifters. We need to rock the boat more and realize there is always room for improvement, even if something has always been done a certain way.

This brings me back to the idea of perfectionism. I used to be a true perfectionist; I thought everything had to be done "right." I wasted so much time trying to get things perfect that when they weren't, I would get upset. I wrote manuscripts that never saw the light of day because, in my head, they weren't good enough. But the truth is if we keep waiting to share with others, nothing will ever be ready. That was one of the biggest lessons I learned when starting Life in Alignment.

I let go of the idea that everything had to be perfect; it was far from it. But I realized if I never put my stuff out there, no one would see it. I now consider myself a recovering perfectionist, no longer subscribing to the idea that everything *has* to be perfect before it's considered complete. I'm over trying to please others, including myself.

Which reminds me, I'm also a former people-pleaser. I grew up trying to live up to my mother's expectations. I never wanted anyone to be mad at me. I spent decades bending over backward, trying to please everyone else. It wasn't until my spiritual awakening that I realized I only needed to please myself. I couldn't make everyone happy, and neither can you. There will always be someone out there who doesn't agree with you, and that's OK! Stop trying to please everyone else because no matter how hard you try, you won't always succeed. Everyone has different opinions and beliefs.

It's time to stop categorizing people based on their religions, cultures, and political beliefs. We are all human; we all live on this planet together. Find a few people to put in your corner who will cheer you on no matter what and leave the rest out. And just because someone doesn't agree with you doesn't mean you have to write them off completely, either.

We need to stop constantly fighting and defending our beliefs. We need to understand that we are all unique and have different experiences that shape our opinions and leave it at that. Everyone is right *and* wrong all the time; it's just a matter of perspective. When we are fighting with others, it is usually our egos that are flaring up. It's the soul that willingly accepts the situation as it, notices the lessons that need to be learned, and then moves on.

Now, let's get back to the idea of rewilding, of slowing down and getting back to our souls. It's important you reconnect with the divine that is within you. Do what brings you joy. You don't have to justify it or explain it to anyone else.

The only rule in my house is "Do no harm." You can do or say whatever you want as long as you don't harm another person mentally, physically, or emotionally in the process. Also, do no harm to the environment you are in; leave the place a little bit better than when you found it.

When we hold on to negative energy, it becomes suppressed and can manifest as illnesses and physical ailments in our bodies. We were taught at a young age that it's not OK to cry or be emotional. This is just as true for men as it is for women. I was an emotionally sensitive young girl growing up and was made fun of by my own family every time my eyes started to tear up. "Oh, Courtney is crying again" was a common phrase in my house. But the truth was I was highly empathic; I felt other people's pain and emotions as if they were my own. A good book or movie can still bring me to tears because I can connect with the characters on such a raw, emotional level.

When I became an adult, however, I started to suppress my emotions. I held a lot of things in. I didn't want to be the emotional young girl at work, not where I wanted respect. But then, I started to get stressed out and experience anxiety. I often let my emotions build up inside of me without releasing them until I would explode like a pressure cooker. I would spend an entire day crying. Any little thing would set me off again, and the water works would start back up.

Back in 2012, I took an herbal class, and I remember my instructor talking about a book called *Feelings Buried Alive Never Die*, which talks about this same idea, the idea that we keep emotions deeply suppressed within us when we don't let them flow out.

Think of our emotions as energetic currents. When we get angry, that energy starts to arise within us. We are often compelled to hit something or scream, and if we allow ourselves to get it out in a healthy way, we often feel better afterward. Same goes for grief or sadness; when we let ourselves cry it out, we might feel energetically drained afterward, but the sadness is lifted.

When a problem is bothering us and we find ourselves talking about it to anyone within ear shot, we often feel better. After talking through the problem, it no longer has as much meaning for us as before. It bothers us a little less because we've been able to energetically let that problem go by putting it out into the universe with our words.

When we are in touch with our emotions and let them rise up and out of us, we often get over our problems more quickly and we are able to move forward sooner. When we hold on to grudges and traumatic experiences, they tend to creep back into our lives and haunt us.

As a society, we've held on to the belief that we need to keep everything to ourselves for too long. I, for one, can't keep a secret. Don't tell me anything you don't want other people to know because I've been an open book my entire life. I will tell you anything you want to know. But that's always been my way of dealing with things. I've always allowed any emotions I have to come up and out. I've never been one to hold things in, and that's just my nature. I realize this might not ring true for everyone, especially those of you who have held on to so many things for so many years, whether out of fear of judgement or shame. I encourage each and every one of you to start journaling or find someone to talk to.

If you don't like sharing your issues with other people, that's OK, but to heal and move forward, you must get all of that icky energetic gunk out of you in some way. This is why I love writing in a journal. It allows me to freely and confidentially explore my thoughts and feelings. A journal is for your eyes only, and it doesn't really matter the modality in which you work through those pent-up emotions. Write them out, talk about them, or take up running or kickboxing. Work through them in whatever way works best for you.

Reflection Questions:

◊ What negative habits do you need to unlearn?

◊ What beliefs do you carry from childhood that no longer resonate with you?

◊ Do you currently express yourself without inhibitions?

◊ How can you become more wild and free?

Lesson 16

Overcoming Fear

Today's Affirmation:

I am fearless. I will no longer let fear
stop me from living my truth.

Fear is a debilitating force. It can stop us cold in our tracks. One moment, we are jazzed about starting a new project and can feel the excitement coursing through our veins as we envision the possibilities, and then, in the next moment, we are talking ourselves out of it. We fear failure and what other people might think of us if we put ourselves out there. We start to see all of the ways our ideas might not work. This is fear at its finest, doing its job to stop us at any given moment.

Our fears prevent us from making progress in our lives. We think to ourselves, *What do I know about X, Y, or Z? Who am I to start a business I know nothing about? I will never be able to afford to quit my day job and live my dream.*

Fear is something that stems from our ego selves. It produces thoughts that aren't actually true. When we feed those fears, we give them the power to take over our lives. It becomes difficult to change our patterns when we start to believe all the things we "think" we are afraid of.

The universal language is love. Love is the opposite of fear and hate. Love is what moves mountains. Love is what makes the world go 'round.

You've heard all of this before, but it's usually not until you are on the other side of a spiritual awakening that you can really see it and feel it. When we choose to let go of fear and vibrate at a higher frequency, we can see we are all in this together.

Franklin D. Roosevelt said, "The only thing we have to fear is fear itself," and he was right. When we are conscious of our fears and ego trying to keep us from moving forward, we can easily work around those blocks. We can see the old stories and patterns that are coming up and simply wish them well and send them on their way.

Your higher self, that soul self we keep talking about, has no fear because it knows everything is going to work out for your highest good. Every test, every limit, and every obstacle that is put in front of you is there to help you grow and learn.

There is no such thing as failure. All of life is an experiment. You have to remind yourself that all the people you look up to in your life had to start somewhere, and I guarantee they were all afraid of something at one time or another. Fear is a part of life. It's a valid emotion when our survival depends on it, but we don't have to give in to it and let it drag us down.

So let's take some time today to look fear in the face. What is stopping you from moving forward and living your dream life? What are you afraid might or might not happen?

One of the best things my mother ever taught me was to pursue everything I want. She would always say, "What's the worst they can say? No?" And she was right! If you asked for something and got told no, that only means you are right back where you started. No, you didn't gain anything, but you didn't lose either. Maybe it means you weren't quite ready for what you asked for yet, maybe you need to work a little bit harder and prove you actually want it, or maybe you need to take a different course of action.

Whatever it is that is stopping you, look at it for what it is. It's your ego trying to keep you from being your biggest and brightest self. Say "Thank you ego for always trying to protect me, but I'm ready for the next best thing."

Reflection Questions:

◊ What fears do you have when it comes to your growth and evolution?

◊ Do you find yourself repeating the same patterns in your life? If so, why do you think that is?

◊ What steps can you take to overcome those fears?

Lesson 17

Astrology as a Tool for Self-Discovery

Today's Affirmation:

I choose to know myself and
love the light and dark parts equally.

Ever since I can remember, I've been intrigued by astrology and my horoscope. Sometimes the daily advice made no sense at all, as I was just a girl and couldn't relate to any "real world" problems at the time. I usually took it with a grain of salt; it was just something fun to look at in the newspaper as my dad read the headlines for the day with his breakfast.

In my adult years, with the help of smartphones, I downloaded a horoscope app so I could have it at my fingertips whenever I wanted to see what the stars had in store for me.

Now, horoscopes are all fine and good for a bit of fun, but what most people don't know is that your natal astrological birth chart holds *a lot* more information as to who you really are as a person.

Most people know their sun sign, which is based on the day you're born. For example, I am a Pisces, meaning the sun was in the sign of Pisces on the day I was born. What most people don't realize is your sun sign is only one part of a much bigger puzzle. Your sun sign is a basic interpretation of who you are, but you, of course, are a complex being, and it's important to at least know your moon sign, rising sign, and midheaven as well.

The sign the moon was in the moment you were born plays a significant role in how you feel emotionally and how you cope with those emotions. It represents the inner you. Your moon sign tends to be the ruling force over your decision-making; it's what you look for to feel secure.

Your rising sign is how people perceive you in public. This is the persona you possess when interacting with strangers. So even though your sun sign might be Aries, your rising sign may be Gemini, meaning you might act one way in public and entirely different at home.

And then, there is your midheaven. This is a point on your natal chart that shows how you *want* to be perceived in society. For example, I have a midheaven in Capricorn, which means I want to be taken seriously. I have an innate fear of being seen as a fraud or not being respected in my profession, which is probably why I've worked so hard all my life to prove myself.

I encourage you to pull up your natal birth chart online. All you need to know is the date, time, and place you were born. The time zone you were born in will affect certain points in your chart as well. You can get a free analysis or find websites that can go into detail on each point in your chart.

One last piece of information to look at when you pull up your natal chart is the north and south nodes. The north node represents your soul purpose. It's your karmic path, where you are heading in this lifetime. It's the future you've been trying to get toward but have struggled with. The south node is in the opposite sign of the north node, and it represents everything we've brought with us in this lifetime. It's our comfort zone and instincts, the past, what feels safe and secure for us. It represents the things we have already mastered. Sometimes where we have been (south node) and where we are aiming to go (north node) can be at odds. I encourage you to do some deep diving into this area of your chart to see what lies ahead for you on your journey in this lifetime.

Before I get too ahead of myself, I encourage you to find out what your sun, moon, rising (also called ascendant), and midheaven signs are first. With just this information alone, you might start to paint a bigger picture of your life.

The natal chart is also divided into twelve houses, and which planets are in those houses will also play a role in your life's work. And, of course, each planet will be in a different sign in your chart, which will clue you in to aspects of your personality, worldview, and life path. How much you want to dive into this information is up to you.

When you are reading other people's interpretations of your natal chart, take everything that applies to you and leave the rest. There are several different interpretations that can be found online, and they are not all going to pertain to you.

The point of this exercise is to get to know yourself more. Know your strengths and lean into your weaknesses. Imagine where you are heading in this lifetime with an open mind. Be curious. Radical self-discovery is the path toward growth and expansion. It's the only way I've found I can easily move on from my mistakes.

By getting to know ourselves more and finding out why we do the things we do, we can become more forgiving toward ourselves and others. We can recognize we are all on this same life path together, trying to figure it out. You will be more understanding when someone snaps at you because you can see they are struggling inside and don't have a way to properly cope with what is going on.

We become more understanding of our fellow beings when we get to know ourselves and learn more about our own psychological behaviors. We have more compassion for others. And when we dive into self-discovery like this, we are able to see the bigger picture. We are able to let go of the small, minute details that bother us and realize the only path forward is to quit repeating the same cycles over and over.

Reflection Questions:

Step 1: Look up your natal astrological chart for free online.

◊ What is your sun sign, moon sign, and rising sign?

◊ Where is your midheaven?

◊ What are your north and south nodes?

Step 2: Find interpretations of what your placements mean for you. What new insights have you discovered about yourself?

Lesson 18

Shadow Work

Today's Affirmation:

I am whole.

Your shadow self is your subconscious. It's the part of yourself you tend to ignore and suppress, and it's the part of you that drives your actions without you being fully aware of it.

People often get put off by talking about shadow work and diving into the dark parts of themselves. It's important to recognize, though, that the darkness within us is not evil; it's not something to fear.

Your shadow self can sometimes include the part of yourself you were taught to put away when you were younger; it can be the things you are secretly interested in but feel ashamed to talk about.

For a lot of people, sexuality is something that's connected with their shadow self, something they want to hide, especially before the LGBTQ+ movement and the legalization of gay marriage.

But it could also be a quirky habit of yours—hell, even a kinky one. Your shadow self is reserved for your eyes only. What is it in your life you have difficulty letting other people see?

The shadow self is often not recognized by the conscious ego. We like to put these parts of ourselves in a box and throw away the key. But what if we tended to these parts of ourselves with love and compassion? What if we accepted them for what they were?

There are oftentimes beautiful gems that are uncovered when we work with our shadow selves, a form of priceless self-acceptance.

Now, I'm not saying you have to tell the world about the parts of yourself you've suppressed for so long, but I do suggest you sit with those things and explore the dark, hidden areas of your personality and life, the things you've always tried to hide and ignore.

Shadow work is not easy by any means. In fact, it's really brutal. Shadow work will strip you down, tear down all the walls you've ever built, and let the floodgates open to pass traumas you wish you didn't have to relive.

The more you've suppressed over the years, the more you might need to work through. I suggest taking it one thing at a time.

If you have intimacy problems, ask yourself why. Go into your shadow self and see where the source of the discomfort lies. If you find yourself repeating the same patterns and cycles over and over again, that may also be a sign that you need to go into your shadow self. Is there a part of you that is self-sabotaging the outcome? Why do you keep repeating these patterns of behavior? Is there a part of you that thrives on the drama and chaos? Are you afraid of what the outcome might be if you really do succeed or move past this cycle?

These are just a few of the questions we can ask ourselves when we begin to do our shadow work. And they can be applied to any area of our lives.

When we start to uncover all these rejected and disowned parts of ourselves, we are able to heal, grow, and expand. I don't believe we all came into this life to set up shop and be done with it; there is always something new to learn and explore, whether that's a physical place or our inner selves. The sky is the limit when it comes to self-discovery.

When you are ready to start exploring your shadow self, take it easy and start slow. Approach it from a place of grace. Don't be hard on yourself. Don't judge yourself. Allow whatever comes up to come through on its own time and agenda. This is not something to force. Not all of us are ready to face our shadow selves all at once.

I promise you the rewards, freedom, release of judgement and fear, healing, growth, and strength you find on the other side is just the tip of the iceberg.

Reflection Questions:

◊ What parts of yourself do you tend to hide away from others? Why? How do you feel when you think about sharing these parts of yourself with others?

◊ What emotions have you been avoiding?

◊ How can you shed light on your shadows? How can you bring the subconscious to the conscious?

Lesson 19

The Divine Feminine

Today's Affirmation:

I am a beautiful soul
shining my light onto the world.

Just as we are all made up of light and dark, we also have masculine and feminine energy within us that is available at any given moment. The entire planet operates on a balanced ecosystem. The problem with the feminine energy in our world, however, is that we don't operate in it as much as we operate in the masculine.

Masculine energy is action-oriented. When we are in our masculine energy, we are logical thinkers, looking for things to do, problems to fix, and to-do lists to attack. When we are in our feminine energy, we are more laid-back and receptive; we feel more connected to our emotions because we are working in a state of flow.

Feminine energy is where we find our creativity because, as we've learned, to be creative, you have to be able to surrender to the flow of things and let whatever appears to take form.

Our Western culture is built on being in the masculine all the time. For centuries, women have been shamed for their feelings, outbursts, and whimsical ideas; women are rarely ever taken seriously.

What we have to realize is that there are benefits to being in each state of energy. The masculine has its benefits just as much as the feminine does, and this applies to all of us living on this planet. We need to learn to incorporate more of the feminine energy into our daily lives so we can maintain balance.

We experience so much anxiety and stress living in the modern, Western world because we feel we need to constantly be in a state of doing something to play catch up with those around us. We think we have to keep hustling and busting our asses to be successful, but the truth is we are depriving ourselves of the feminine when we do this.

There is relief when we are in our feminine energy. Worries and anxiety tend to flow away because we let them. Yes, being in the feminine can bring up more emotions, but they flow out just as easily as they flow in.

I like to associate the feminine with the ocean. In mythology and symbolism, the feminine has long been associated with the moon and its cycles, which, as we've discussed, syncs with our menstrual cycles.

Picture the ocean, just for a moment. The waves rise and fall, the tide comes in and goes back out. There are hurricanes and storms, but it can also be calm and peaceful. The feminine, much like the ocean, is all about riding the waves of life.

By living in the masculine all the time, though, we are trying to put that ocean into a box. We are forcing something down to behave in a way that wasn't meant for us. The ocean needs its room to expand and contract in the same way we need space to experience all of our emotions. It's important that we have our masculine and feminine energies in harmonious balance.

This idea of divine feminine is grounded in spirituality. To bring order back to our world, we must reclaim the feminine energy that was suppressed so long ago. Accessing the divine feminine within you is the same as awakening the Shakti and tapping into that creative, life force energy, which we experienced in Lesson 8.

The feminine is nurturing. Think of archetypes like the Mother or Priestess. We need to stop competing with each other in the ego-driven masculine and start connecting with one another in our feminine.

We are all a part of this web of life. We all play our role. Each of us has a unique purpose, and it's up to us to share those gifts, to be so divinely aligned and authentic in an energetically balanced way.

Before monotheistic religions took over, people used to worship gods and goddesses alike; each one played a role. The feminine was honored for her gifts. The mother, in particular, was honored for bringing life into the world.

Women used to be oracles and priestesses until men pushed them out and made up excuses to keep them out of temples.

The truth is we are all on this planet together. We are all part of the divine, and the divine is a part of each and every one of us. Those goosebumps you get when you meditate, feel a breeze against your skin, or connect so deeply to lyrics in a song is the divine speaking to you. That is your soul recognizing something spiritual in that moment.

It's time to recognize and honor not only women but the feminine energy within all of us. We need to stop telling our boys it's not OK to cry, that they need to "toughen up" or "be a man." Emotions are a part of the human experience. We can all relate to them because we all feel them.

Reflection Questions:

◊ Do you spend most of your day in your masculine or feminine energy?

◊ Take a piece of paper and make two columns. One side for masculine and one side for feminine. Now, list all the attributes and words that come up for you when you think about their different energies.

◊ How can you incorporate more of your masculine/ feminine energies into your routine so you feel more balanced?

◊ Is there anything off-putting to you about harnessing your feminine energy? Why? What triggers you?

Lesson 20

Working with Goddesses

Today's Affirmation:

I am a goddess, and
I deserve to be treated as such.

Working with goddesses is one of the best ways to open yourself up to the divine feminine. Each goddess has her own attributes, personalities, and archetypes. We can pick and choose which ones we are drawn to at any time.

To reclaim the feminine within us, we have to start believing we are goddesses ourselves because we are. If the divine resides with you, then you are a goddess. You carry divinity, you have the ability to create life, and you can access the power of Shakti.

Working with goddesses is just another modality to explore more about ourselves. Each goddess I've opened up to and worked with has taught me something new about myself.

Take, for example, one of my personal favorite goddesses, Hekate, the Greek Goddess of the Crossroads and Queen of the Witches. When I first opened up to Hekate, she packed a powerful punch. Her energy was strong, and I could feel her all around me. The most beautiful lesson she taught me was to believe in my own power. She reminded me that I was magic and could create any life I wanted to live. As Goddess of the Crossroads, she was great for guiding me on the right path, and I experienced all of that after working with her for just one hour!

Hekate is also a dark goddess and can help us work through a lot of anger and wrongdoings that have been done to us as women—not just in this lifetime but past lives as well. I've since opened up to her and sought out her guidance many times over the years.

At Life in Alignment, I've created different workshops to help you tap into the energy of different goddesses. I want women to be able to have the same experiences I've had if they are open and willing. Each of the goddess workshops I create have different guided meditations to bring you into the right energy. All you have to do is be willing to open up.

Be open to the possibilities. Be open to the gifts each goddess wants to share with you. Allow them to take you on a journey of self-discovery. Let them help you heal old wounds and past traumas.

If you are struggling being intimate with a partner or find you are struggling with your self-worth, call on Aphrodite, the Goddess of Love, to help guide you. The Hindu Goddess of Death and Destruction Kali Ma is, in my experience, the destroyer of egos. If you find yourself getting in your own way or you need a good firm push in the right direction, call on this goddess.

Artemis is the Huntress, the Wild Woman. As the Greek Goddess of the Wild and the Hunt, she helps us stay true to our goals. Artemis reminds us that we are all wild and it's OK to live like so. There is no need to subscribe to the cultural norms. She beckons us to get outside and reconnect with nature and our true, wild selves.

Athena is the Warrior Goddess. Her sword cuts through the bullshit, and she reminds us that, with strategy and confidence, we can face anything that stands in our way.

In no particular order, here is a short list of goddesses you have the potential to work with:

◊ Persephone, Queen of the Underworld (Greek)

◊ Demeter, Goddess of the Harvest (Greek)

◊ Athena, Goddess of Wisdom and Strategy (Greek)

◊ Artemis, Goddess of the Wilderness(Greek)

◊ Aphrodite, Goddess of Love, Art, and Beauty (Greek)

◊ Hekate, Goddess of the Crossroads, Queen of Witches (Greek)

◊ Diana, Goddess of the Moon and the Hunt (Roman)

◊ Vesta, Goddess of Hearth, Home, and Fire (Roman)

◊ Kali Ma, Goddess of Death and Destruction (Hindu)

◊ Parvati, Goddess of Love and Devotion (Hindu)

◊ Cerridwen, Goddess of Fertility, Knowledge, and Poetry (Celtic)

◊ Sophia, Goddess of Wisdom (Hebrew)

◊ Morgan le Fay, Priestess of Avalon (Celtic)

◊ Brigid, Goddess of Fire, Healer, Poets, and Smiths (Celtic)

◊ Tara, Goddess of Healing and Compassion (Hindu)

◊ Saraswati, Goddess of the Arts (Hindu)

◊ Lakshmi, Goddess of Good Fortune (Hindu)

◊ Isis, Goddess of Magic, Fertility, and Motherhood (Egyptian)

◊ Freya, Goddess of Love, Beauty, and Fertility (Norse)

◊ Lilith, Goddess of Equality and Independence (Jewish)

◊ Pele, Goddess of Fire and Volcanos (Hawaiian)

◊ Gaia, Goddess of the Earth (Greek)

◊ Hathor, Goddess of the Sky, Women, and Love (Egyptian)

I could go on and on about goddesses (that's for another day and another book), but the point here is that I encourage you to open up and learn about the different goddesses that call to you. You can even take our free quiz online at www.lifein-alignment. com/quiz to see which one speaks to you at any given time.

And, of course, who you turn to depends on where you are in life and what you are currently dealing with. One day, you might be ovulating and feel called to explore your sensual side with Aphrodite, and the next day, you might have to make a big presentation at work in a room full of men with Athena by your side.

There is no right or wrong way to call on a goddess. Let your intuition guide you. Reading books on mythology, purchasing a goddess oracle deck, hopping on Pinterest, or conducting a simple internet search on goddesses will suffice.

But know that when we start working with goddess energy, we unlock parts of ourselves. We connect with and honor the goddesses in our own ways. Just be open and willing to receive, as that is the feminine way.

By exploring archetypes and different goddesses, I have awakened those archetypes within myself. I consider myself to be an introverted, highly sensitive, and deeply caring person, so for me, I am not in the warrior mentality that often. Sometimes I muse around with the Lover and the Wild Woman, but my prominent archetypes are the Mother, the Dark Goddess, and the Priestess.

There are many different faces to the goddesses, but I think the most common ones I see women work with are the Mother, the Lover, the Dark Goddess, the Witch, and the Warrior. Each one comes with her own double-edged sword.

For example, women often hold a lot of wounds when it comes to working with the Mother archetype. You might have grown up without a mother or had one that was physically, mentally, or emotionally abusive. I know, for me, I had to work through this idea of striving to live up to my mother's expectations of me. They might have all been in my head and I'm sure my own mother would deny them, but I had to ultimately learn to forgive my mother for not being the mother I needed her to be.

As a mother now, I make mistakes on a regular basis, and it's a lot easier to realize that my own mother was coping with parenting and learning as she went along, doing the best she knew how. Still, there were a lot of things she could have done differently to nurture and support me more emotionally. For starters, she could have sat me down and had a conversation with me about puberty and sex, which was something I had to learn from my peers and sex education class in school. While my mom was a nurse and constantly walked around naked in our home, unafraid of her own body (she would always say "There's nothing I have that you don't," and of course, this would work in a house full of women), she struggled a lot with her self-image.

As an adult, I can now forgive and move past the mistakes of my childhood, but it took some work with the Mother archetype and my own inner child to heal from it.

The Witch archetype is another one that's close to my heart. The Witch wound is so common in our society, but it's rarely discussed or talked about. It stems from centuries of women's suppression. Women were once the healers and wise women of the villages, but fear from the patriarchy caused men to turn on them and prosecute them as witches and heretics.

Women had to learn to go underground to work with herbs and natural remedies. No longer was it safe for women to meet in groups because it was believed that if women got together, they would start to form "wild ideas."

Only in the last few decades has it been OK to come out and proclaim yourself a witch without fear of persecution. There has been an ingrained fear in us that we karmically brought into this lifetime because of all the hysteria and widespread witch trials that were done in the 1400s and 1500s in Europe.

I think the witch trials during that time also severed our relationship with nature. Organized religion was trying so desperately to gain control of the people that it adopted some of the most popular pagan gods and goddesses and made them saints. Holidays were created around pagan traditions; Yuletide became known as Christmas, Ostara was renamed Easter, and Samhain became Halloween.

The wise women of the villages were long forgotten, and word spread that people needed an experienced male physician to help cure their ailments instead.

I could go on and on about archetypes and goddesses, but I've compiled a short list to help you start thinking about them. These come from the work I've done with other women, Jungian psychology (Carl Jung popularized the concept of archetypes), and my own research.

The five common feminine archetypes I see women work with are:

◊ Mother

◊ Lover

◊ Dark Goddess

◊ Warrior

◊ Medicine Woman/Witch

For those interested in the seven feminine Jungian archetypes:

◊ Maiden

◊ Mother

◊ Lover

◊ Mystic

◊ Queen

◊ Huntress

◊ Wise Woman

Other archetypes worth mentioning are:

◊ Priestess/Oracle

◊ Midwife

◊ Awakener

◊ Storyteller

◊ Visionary

◊ Siren

Reflection Questions:

◊ Which goddess do you feel called to learn more about in this moment?

◊ Is there anything that triggers you when you think about yourself as a goddess?

◊ What two prominent archetypes do you see in yourself?

Lesson 21

Reflections

Today's Affirmation:

_____

_____

(Create your own!)

I want you to take time in this lesson to hit pause and reflect on your journey over the last twenty-one days.

Which lessons resonated with you the most? Were there any lessons that triggered you? Were there any lessons you had a harder time working with? If so, why?

These answers aren't for me; they are for you. They are to help you recognize parts of your journey that, perhaps, you need to spend more time with or let go of entirely.

What are you curious about and would like to expand your knowledge on? How will you continue your daily spiritual practice? Have you noticed a difference in the way you respond to things in your life? Has there been a difference in the way you've felt or the way you wake up every morning?

I hope you can take all the information in this book and apply it to your life. I hope it makes you rethink how you view yourself and the world around you.

We all chose to come on this planet at this time to live this human experience and make the most of it. Life is not meant to be wasted away watching Netflix every evening and keeping yourself locked inside.

The world is a big place, and I hope you find your little piece of heaven within it. I hope you find peace within yourself.

The road to healing and self-discovery is a long one, but I think the more we understand ourselves, our triggers and shortcomings, and why we do the things we do, the more love and compassion we can then have for other people. We will be able to better understand where they are coming from, and we can have more empathy for those who are struggling and acting out.

It's so easy to get wrapped up in other people's drama, but knowing that you are ultimately responsible for your thoughts and actions makes the world seem a little bit easier to navigate. It's not your job to fix anyone else; it's only your job to take care of you.

Take all the noise and advice you read and hear to your inner flame. Discern for yourself what is true for you and leave the rest behind. We are all unique and on different paths, so whatever you come across on social media might be for you, and it might not. Don't ever let anyone tell you what you should and shouldn't do—not even me.

The reflection questions at the end of each chapter were meant to provoke thought and get you to ask more questions, and I hope you continue to do so.

I hope you understand that you are beautiful and unique and you don't have to carry the weight of the world on your shoulders. I hope you've learned something new about yourself and that you take your newfound curiosity and continue to explore.

Don't ever stop on the ever-winding journey to your soul.

Reflection Questions:

◊ What lessons did you find most helpful?

◊ Were there any lessons you could spend more time on?

◊ How has your viewpoint changed after reading this book?

◊ What is your affirmation?

Acknowledgments

It really does take a village to bring a book to life and I couldn't have done it without my supportive tribe. One must always have people in their corner to cheer them on.

I first want to thank my husband Ryan, for always supporting me and giving me time and space to work on my dreams.

Thank you to Gina Johnson and Jennifer Colosky for all your support and reading the first draft of this book. Your encouragement kept me going.

Thanks to my editor Lyric Dodson for turning my jumbled mess into the polished work we get to read today. I'm so lucky our paths crossed at just the right time.

Thank you to Mandi Lynn for the cover design and putting up with my multiple changes and ideas.

Thank you to all the amazing Light Leaders who helped me birth this baby out into the world: Lyndsey Gootee, Karlyn Langjhar, Madilyn Smith, Annette Szproch, Lydia Elias, Jillian Grover, Lais Cerutti Scortegagna, Gina Lamson, Nicole MacDonald, Kristine Rodriguez, Morgan Dahl, Stephanie Johnson, LaToya Roux, Barbara Siemen, and the rest of the TAA sisterhood. I'm so lucky to have each of you beautiful women in my corner with your endless support and encouragement.

And to all the others involved in the Journey to Soul Street Team! Thank you for all your hard work!

Stay Connected

You can find Courtney Tiffany on:
Facebook: @authorcourtneytiffany
Instagram: @authorcourtneytiffany
Pinterest: @monthly_goddess_circle
Patreon: @authorcourtneytiffany

Sign up for Courtney's Monthly Author Newsletter and be the first
to hear about her upcoming projects:
www.courtneytiffany.com

If you've enjoyed this book, please consider leaving a review on
Amazon or Goodreads.